# KIDNA

The years after 1745 were ~~unhappy~~ time for Scotland. The Highlanders had fought against King George of England, and lost, and now his soldiers were driving many Highlanders out of their homes.

David Balfour is from the Scottish Lowlands and is not worried by the English soldiers. When he leaves his home to begin a new life, he is not looking for trouble and danger. But trouble quickly comes to him. He meets his rich uncle, who is not at all pleased to learn that he has a poor nephew. One danger follows another, and David finds himself in the Highlands, where he meets Alan Breck, a proud Stewart. The Stewarts hate both the English and the Campbells, who work for King George, so Alan is a dangerous friend for David to have.

Then murder is done, and David and Alan are on the run for their lives across the mountains . . .

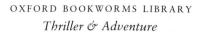

OXFORD BOOKWORMS LIBRARY
*Thriller & Adventure*

# Kidnapped

Stage 3 (1000 headwords)

Series Editor: Jennifer Bassett
Founder Editor: Tricia Hedge
Activities Editors: Jennifer Bassett and Christine Lindop

ROBERT LOUIS STEVENSON

# Kidnapped

## The Adventures of David Balfour
## in the Year 1751

*Retold by*
Clare West

*Illustrated by*
Chris Koelle

OXFORD UNIVERSITY PRESS

# OXFORD
UNIVERSITY PRESS

Great Clarendon Street, Oxford OX2 6DP

Oxford University Press is a department of the University of Oxford.
It furthers the University's objective of excellence in research, scholarship,
and education by publishing worldwide in

Oxford New York

Auckland Cape Town Dar es Salaam Hong Kong Karachi
Kuala Lumpur Madrid Melbourne Mexico City Nairobi
New Delhi Shanghai Taipei Toronto

With offices in

Argentina Austria Brazil Chile Czech Republic France Greece
Guatemala Hungary Italy Japan Poland Portugal Singapore
South Korea Switzerland Thailand Turkey Ukraine Vietnam

OXFORD and OXFORD ENGLISH are registered trade marks of
Oxford University Press in the UK and in certain other countries

This simplified edition © Oxford University Press 2008

Database right Oxford University Press (maker)

First published in Oxford Bookworms 1995

2 4 6 8 10 9 7 5 3 1

Any websites referred to in this publication are in the public domain and
their addresses are provided by Oxford University Press for information only.
Oxford University Press disclaims any responsibility for the content

ISBN 978 0 19 479120 5

Typeset by Wyvern Typesetting Ltd, Bristol

Printed in Hong Kong

ACKNOWLEDGEMENTS
*Illustrated by:* Chris Koelle/Portland Studios, Greenville, USA

Word count (main text): 12,435 words

For more information on the Oxford Bookworms Library,
visit www.oup.com/elt/bookworms

# CONTENTS

# 1
## David meets his uncle

It was early in the month of June, 1751, when I shut the door of our house behind me for the last time. All my life I had lived in the quiet little village of Essendean, in the Lowlands of Scotland, where my father had been the dominie, or schoolteacher. But now that he and my mother were both dead, I had to leave the house. The new dominie would soon arrive, and *he* would teach at the school and live in the dominie's house. So, although I was only seventeen, there was nowhere for me to live, and no reason for me to stay in Essendean.

*I shut the door behind me for the last time.*

1

But my heart was beating with excitement as I walked down the road, because in my hand I carried the letter that my father had given me just before he died. 'Davie,' he had said, 'when I am dead, take this to the house of Shaws, near Cramond. That's where I came from, and that's where you must go. Put this letter into the hands of Ebenezer Balfour.'

Balfour! The same name as my own! It was the first time I had heard of any of our family outside Essendean.

So I decided to walk to Cramond, hoping that perhaps this Mr Balfour, in his fine big house, would receive me kindly, and help me to become a rich man one day. With my plaid over my shoulder, I walked fast up the hill away from the village. What an adventure, to leave that sleepy place, where nothing ever happened, and go to a great, busy house, to be with rich and important people of my own name and blood! But when I reached the top of the hill, I turned a little sadly, to take my last look at the dominie's house, and Essendean churchyard, where my father and mother lay.

My journey northwards took almost two days. By midday on the second day I could see the smoking chimneys of Edinburgh in front of me, and soon I arrived in Cramond.

Now I began to ask people on the road for the house of Shaws. Their answers worried me a little. Some people seemed surprised, some afraid, and some angry, when I spoke the name of Ebenezer Balfour. I could not understand this, but it was too far to go back to Essendean that day, and I wanted to find the rest of the Balfour family very much. So I continued on my way, and when I met a dark, wild-looking

*I took my last look at Essendean churchyard.*

woman coming towards me, I asked her where the house of Shaws was. She took me to the top of the next hill, and showed me a large building standing alone in the bottom of the next valley. Although the fields around were green, and the farmland was excellent, the house itself looked unfinished and empty. Part of its roof was missing. There was no road to it, and no smoke coming from any of its chimneys, nor was there any garden.

'That!' I cried. 'No, it can't be!'

'It is!' cried the woman angrily. 'That is the house of Shaws! Blood built it, blood stopped the building of it, and blood shall bring it down! Black is the heart of Ebenezer Balfour! Ye can tell him from me that I hope to see him die, and his house fall down around him!'

The woman turned and disappeared. I stood where she left me, shaking like a leaf, and looking down at the house for a long time. But when it began to get dark, I noticed some smoke coming out of the chimney, and felt a little more hopeful. 'There must be a fire, and cooking, and people in the house,' I thought. So I walked up to the front door. The house seemed locked up and unwelcoming, but there was firelight shining through the kitchen window, and I could hear someone talking quietly to himself. Bravely, I lifted my hand and knocked loudly on the strong wooden door. The house was suddenly silent, and there was no reply. I knocked and knocked, and shouted as loudly as I could. Finally, the window opened, and a man holding a gun put his head out.

'What do ye want?' he asked.

'I've come here with a letter for Mr Ebenezer Balfour of Shaws. Is he here?'

'Who is it from?' asked the man with the gun.

'That's none of your business,' I replied, getting angry.

'Well, put the letter down by the door, and leave.'

'I will not!' I answered sharply. 'I'm going to give it to Mr Balfour himself. The letter introduces me to him.'

'Who are ye then?' was the next question.

'I'm not ashamed of my name. It's David Balfour.'

The man almost dropped his gun. After a long while, he asked in a changed voice, 'Is your father dead?' I was too surprised to answer, but he continued, 'Aye, he must be dead, and that's why ye have come. Well, man, I'll let ye in,' and he disappeared from the window.

Now the door was unlocked, and a voice from the darkness said, 'Go into the kitchen and touch nothing.' I obeyed, while the man locked the heavy door carefully again. I found myself in the emptiest kitchen that I had ever seen. There was a fire, but no other light. On the table was a bowl of porridge and a glass of water, in front of the only chair. Around the walls were several locked chests. There was no other furniture. The man who now appeared in the kitchen was small, mean-looking and white-faced, between fifty and seventy years old, and wearing a dirty old nightshirt. The worst thing about him was that he could neither take his eyes away from me, nor look straight into my face.

'If ye're hungry,' he said, 'ye can eat that porridge. It's grand food, porridge! Let me see the letter!'

'It's for Mr Balfour, not you,' I replied.

'And who do ye think I am? Give me Alexander's letter! Ye may nót like me or my house or my porridge, but I'm your born uncle, Davie, my man!'

This was the end of all my hopes. I was too tired and miserable to speak, so I silently gave him the letter, and sat down to eat the porridge.

'Your father's been dead a long time?' he asked, giving me a quick look from his sharp eyes.

'Three weeks, sir,' I said.

'He was a secretive man, Alexander was. Perhaps he didn't talk much about me? Or about the house of Shaws?'

'I never knew he had a brother, sir, or ever heard the name of Shaws.'

5

*'Give me Alexander's letter!'*

'To think of that!' he replied. 'A strange man!' But he seemed very pleased, and began to look at me with more interest. Soon he jumped up and said, 'We're going to get on well, Davie! What's mine is yours, man, and what's yours is mine. Blood's thicker than water, and there's only ye and me of the name of Balfour. Now I'll show ye to your bed.'

He took me up some dark stairs and showed me into a room. I could not see anything.

'Can I have a light, sir?' I asked.

'No, ye can't. No lights in this house! I'm afraid of fires, ye see. Good night to ye, Davie, my man.' And before I had time to reply, he pulled the door shut and locked it from the outside. The room was very cold, but luckily I had my plaid with me, so I covered myself with it like a blanket, and soon fell asleep.

The next day my uncle and I had a small bowl of porridge and a glass of water for breakfast, lunch and supper. He did not speak much to me, but was clearly thinking hard. I often noticed him looking at me, while pretending to do something different, and he never left me alone in the kitchen with the locked chests, in which, I supposed, he kept his money. I did not like the way he looked at me, and began to wonder if he was a little crazy, and perhaps dangerous.

After supper he said suddenly, 'Davie, I've been thinking. I promised your father a bit of money for ye before ye were born. A promise is a promise – and so I'm going to give ye . . . forty pounds!' These last words seemed very painful to him. He added, in a kind of scream, 'Scots!'

A Scottish pound was the same as an English shilling. I could see that his story was a lie, so I laughed at him, saying, 'Oh, think again, sir! *English* pounds, surely!'

'That's what I said,' replied my uncle quickly. 'Go outside for a moment, and I'll get the money for ye.'

I was smiling as I went out, sure that he would give me nothing at all. It was a dark night, and I could hear wind in the hills. 'There may be thunder later,' I thought, not knowing how important the weather would be to me that night.

But when my uncle called me in again, he counted thirty-eight English pounds in gold into my hands. It clearly hurt him to do it, and he kept back the last two pounds, but I did not mind that. Surprised and pleased, I thanked him warmly.

'Now,' he said, looking cleverly at me, '*ye* can give *me* something, Davie. I'm getting old now, and I need help.'

'Of course, sir,' I answered. 'What can I do?'

'Well, go outside and climb the stairs at the other end of the house, where the building isn't finished yet. Go up to the room at the top, and bring down the chest that ye'll find there. It's got valuable papers in it.'

'Can I have a light, sir?' I asked.

'No,' he said sharply. 'No lights in my house!'

'Very well, sir. Are the stairs good?'

'They're grand,' said he. 'The stairs are grand.'

Out I went into the night. As I was feeling my way along the outside wall, there was a sudden flash of lightning, then black darkness again. I found the stairs and started climbing. I was about fifteen metres above the ground, when there was another flash of lightning. That was lucky for me, because it showed me that the steps were uneven, and that I could easily fall to my death. 'These are the grand stairs!' I thought. 'Perhaps my uncle wants me to die!' Now I was very careful, and I felt each step with my hands before I put my foot on it. A few steps later my hand felt cold stone, and then nothing more. The stairs ended there, twenty metres above the ground. I felt cold with fear, when I thought of the danger that I had been in. Sending a stranger up those stairs in the dark was sending him straight to his death.

Angrily, I turned and felt my way down. There was a crash of thunder, and suddenly the rain came down. At the bottom of the stairs I looked towards the kitchen, and could see, in the next flash of lightning, a figure standing still in the

*The stairs ended there – I felt cold with fear.*

doorway, listening. When the thunder sounded again, louder than before, he ran back inside, and I followed as softly as I could. I found him sitting in the kitchen, drinking whisky straight from the bottle, and shaking with fear. Quietly I came up behind him, and, putting my hands suddenly on his shoulders, cried, 'Ah!'

My uncle gave a kind of broken cry, and fell to the floor like a dead man. His face was a strange blue colour, and I began to think that he really was dead. At last his eyes opened, and he looked up and saw me. 'Oh man, are ye alive or a ghost?' he cried. 'Get me my medicine, Davie – it's for my heart.' I found the medicine bottle and gave him some. He soon began to look a little better.

'Why did you lie to me?' I asked angrily. 'Why did you give me money? And why did you try to kill me? Answer me!'

'I'll tell ye tomorrow, Davie, I promise. Help me to bed now, will ye?' He still looked very ill, so I could not refuse. But this time I locked *his* bedroom door, and went to sleep in front of the kitchen fire.

When I woke up in the morning, I felt very pleased with myself. 'He thinks he's cleverer than me, but he isn't!' I thought. When I let my uncle out of his room, I asked him again for an explanation. After a while, he said, 'Davie, I have some business with a ship's captain at Queensferry. Now, we could walk over there, and when I've done my business, we could visit the lawyer, Mr Rankeillor. He'll answer all your questions. He's an honest man, and he knew your father. What do ye say to that?'

I thought for a moment. I had never seen the sea, but had always wanted to! 'It's a grand idea,' I said.

It was a morning's walk to Queensferry, which was west of Edinburgh, but we did not say a word to each other on the way. Suddenly, at the top of a hill, we could see the Firth of Forth below us, blue and calm, with white sails on it.

'Ye see that public house?' asked my uncle. 'Captain Hoseason's there, to do business with me. There's the ship's boat on the beach, waiting to take him to the ship. And there's the ship itself! A grand ship!'

I had to agree with him. The sailors were getting the ship ready for sailing, and I thought what an exciting adventure that would be – to sail away to a foreign country.

We walked down the hill to the public house and met the captain there. He was a tall, dark, serious-looking man, who shook hands politely with me. Stupidly, I left these two men to their business, and ran down to the beach, to talk to the sailors and look at the boats. It was all new and very interesting to me.

As I was coming back, I met the owner of the public house. 'Good morning,' he said. 'Did ye come with Ebenezer?'

'I did,' I replied. 'He isn't well liked, I understand.'

'That's true,' he answered. 'Nobody speaks well of him. It all started with that story about Mr Alexander, his brother.'

'*What* story?' I asked.

'Oh, just that Ebenezer had killed him. Did ye never hear that?'

'And why would he kill my f–, I mean, Alexander?'

'To get the house, of course, the house of Shaws.'

'Aye, man? Was my – was Alexander older than Ebenezer?'

'Indeed he was! No other reason for killing him!'

This was a great surprise to me! I had thought that my father was the *younger* brother, and I now understood why my uncle had lied to me, and wanted to kill me. The house of Shaws had belonged to my father, not my uncle, and now I had inherited it. The poor country boy who had walked from Essendean was the owner of a fine house and farmland! My head was full of the wonderful things that I could do in my life, as I looked, unseeing, at the sea.

Just then my uncle and the captain came out of the public house. The captain smiled in a friendly way as he spoke to me. 'Sir,' he said, 'Mr Balfour has told me a lot about ye. I'm only sorry I haven't time to get to know ye better. But I'd like ye to come on to my ship for half an hour, before we sail, and have a drink with me.'

Now, more than anything in the world, I wanted to see the inside of a ship, but I remembered that I had to be careful. 'My uncle and I have to see the lawyer, sir,' I replied, 'so I'm afraid we may not have enough time.'

'Aye, aye,' he answered, 'I know, but ye see, the ship's boat can put ye both down near Rankeillor's house, after ye've seen the ship, so ye won't lose any time.' Suddenly he said quietly in my ear, 'Watch out for the old man – he wants to hurt ye. Come and talk about it.' Putting his arm in mine, he said loudly, 'What can I bring ye back from my travels? A friend of Mr Balfour's is a friend of mine!'

*'Watch out for the old man – he wants to hurt ye.'*

By this time we were on the beach, and he was helping my
uncle and me into the boat. I thought that I had found a good
friend and helper, and I was very excited as we came closer to
the great ship, full of busy, noisy sailors. The captain and I
were the first to climb up the ship's side, and at the top the
captain immediately put his arm through mine and began to
talk about the ship.

'But where is my uncle?' I asked suddenly. I pulled myself
away from the captain's arm, and ran to the side of the ship.
Sure enough, there was the boat returning to Queensferry,
with my uncle sitting in it. I screamed, 'Help, help! Murder!'
and my uncle slowly turned to look at me.

I did not see any more. Already strong hands were pulling
me away. Then something hit my head; I saw a great flash of
fire, and fell to the ground.

# 2
# Kidnapped!

When I woke up in darkness, my head was hurting badly, and I was unable to move my hands or feet. I could hear the sailors' shouts and the sound of the wind and the waves. The whole world seemed to go up, up, up, and then down again. I felt very ill, and at first could not understand what was happening. After a while I realized that I must be somewhere inside the ship, which was moving very fast through the water. 'I've been kidnapped!' I thought angrily. It was clear that my uncle and the captain had planned it together. I began to feel frightened and hopeless, as I lay there in the dark.

Some hours later, a light shone in my face. Mr Riach, one of the ship's officers, stood looking down at me. He washed the cut on my head, gave me some water, and told me kindly to go to sleep. The next time he came, I was feeling very hot and ill. He had brought Captain Hoseason with him.

'Now, sir, see for yourself,' said Mr Riach. 'The lad's seriously ill. We must take him out of this unhealthy hole at once.'

'That's none of your business,' answered the captain. 'Ye're paid to do your job, not worry about the boy. He's staying down here.'

'I'm only paid to be an officer on this ship,' replied Mr Riach sharply. He looked hard at the captain. 'I'm not paid, like you, to kidnap and murder—'

Hoseason turned on him angrily. 'What did ye say?' he cried. 'What do ye mean?'

'You understand,' said Mr Riach, looking calmly at him.

'You should know me by now, Mr Riach. I'm a hard man. But if ye say the lad will die—'

'Aye, he will!' said Mr Riach.

'Well, sir, put him where ye like!'

So I was carried up into the sunlight a few minutes later, and put in a cabin where some of the sailors were sleeping. It was a wonderful feeling to see the daylight and to be able to talk to people again. I lay in the cabin for several days, and after a while began to feel better. The sailors were kind to me in their way. They brought me food and drink, and told me about their families at home. I discovered from them that the ship was sailing to the Carolinas, in North America. There the captain was planning to sell me as a slave, to work in a rich man's house or on a farm.

I also learnt that both the ship's officers, Mr Riach and Mr Shuan, enjoyed drinking far too much. The sailors liked Mr Shuan, but said that he was sometimes violent when he had drunk a lot. One of the sailors was a young boy, called Ransome. His job was to bring meals to the captain and officers in the round-house, a big cabin on the top of the ship, where the officers slept and ate. When Ransome dropped something or did something wrong, Mr Shuan used to hit him, and I often saw the poor boy crying.

One night, about nine o'clock, I heard one of the sailors in the cabin saying quietly to the others, 'Shuan's killed him at last!' We all knew who he meant. Just then the captain came in. I was surprised to see him walk towards me and say kindly, 'My man, we want ye to help us in the round-house. From now on, ye'll sleep there instead of Ransome.' As he spoke, two sailors carried Ransome into the cabin. His face was as white as a sheet, and he did not move. My blood ran cold when I saw him.

I obeyed the captain, and ran to the round-house. It was a large room, with a table, a bench and locked cupboards. All the best food and drink was kept there, under the captain's eye, as well as the guns. When I entered, I saw Mr Shuan sitting at the table, with a bottle of whisky in front of him. He did not seem to notice what was happening around him, and was looking fixedly at the table.

Mr Riach soon joined the captain and me. He looked at Hoseason meaningfully, and I understood from his look that Ransome was dead. We all three stood silently looking down at Mr Shuan.

Suddenly the captain stepped forward. 'Do ye know what ye've done?' he cried. 'Ye've murdered the boy!'

Mr Shuan put a hand to his head. 'Well,' he said, 'he brought me a dirty glass!'

The captain and Mr Riach and I looked at each other, almost frightened. Then Hoseason took Mr Shuan by the arm, and told him to go to bed. The murderer cried a little at first, but he took off his boots and lay down, like a small child.

*We all three stood looking down at Mr Shuan.*

'Mr Riach,' said the captain, when we could see that Mr Shuan was asleep, 'nobody on land must know what happened tonight. We'll say that the boy fell into the sea. Get us a drink, David, we both need one,' and he gave me the key to the cupboards.

In the next few days I was very busy, running here and there with the officers' food and drink. Mr Riach and the captain were surprisingly patient with me when I made mistakes. Perhaps they were thinking of the poor boy who had died. But Mr Shuan was very strange after Ransome's death. He did not seem to know what he had done, or to recognize me. On my second day in the round-house, he looked at me with a white face and fear in his eyes. 'You weren't here before?' he asked.

'No, sir,' I replied.

'There was another boy?' he asked. 'Ah! Yes, I thought so,' and sitting down, he called for some more whisky.

It wasn't a hard life for me. I was able to eat well, and talk to Mr Riach, who spoke to me like a friend. But I could not forget poor Ransome. As the days passed, I became more and more worried. I knew that, when the ship arrived in the Carolinas, I would no longer be a free man, but a slave. I thought hard, but there did not seem to be any way of escaping.

About a week later, we were sailing round the rocky coast of northern Scotland in very bad weather. It was difficult to see anything because of the thick fog. One evening there was a great crash, and the officers ran out to see what had happened. I thought we had hit a rock, but in fact it was a small boat. As we watched, the boat broke in two, and went to the bottom with all its men, except the one passenger. At the moment of the crash, this man managed to jump up and catch the side of the ship and pull himself up.

The captain brought him into the round-house. He was smallish but well-built, with an open, sunburnt face, and bright, amused eyes. When he took off his long coat, I could see that he had a pair of pistols and was wearing a sword at his side. Although his life had clearly been in great danger, he seemed very calm, and spoke politely to the captain. Hoseason was looking with interest at the man's clothes. He was wearing a hat with feathers, a blue coat with silver buttons, and expensive-looking lace round his neck.

'I'm sorry about the boat, sir,' said the captain.

'I've lost some grand friends today,' replied the stranger, 'and that's worse than losing ten boats.'

'Well, sir, there are more men in the world than boats,' replied the captain, still watching him closely. 'I know, because *I've been in France, like you.*'

He said these last words clearly and carefully. They seemed to have a special meaning. The stranger put his hand quickly on his pistol.

'Don't worry,' said Hoseason. 'Ye've a French soldier's coat on your back and a Scottish tongue in your head, that's true, but so has many an honest man these days.'

'Well, sir,' replied the stranger, 'I must tell you that I'm one of those honest Highlanders who were proud to fight for their homes, their clan and their country in 1745, against the English King. And I must tell you another thing. If King George's soldiers find me, I'll be in trouble. I was on my way to France, where some of my clansmen live now. But in the fog my boat missed the French ship that was meeting me. So if you can take me to France, I'll pay you well.'

He opened his purse and showed that it was full of gold coins. The captain seemed excited as he looked at the money, and then at the man's face.

'If you can take me to France, I'll pay you well.'

'To France?' he replied. 'No, I can't do that. But to the Highlands, aye, we can discuss that.' They sat down together, and in the end agreed that the captain would take the stranger to Loch Linnhe, on the north-west coast of Scotland, for sixty pounds. There the Highlander would be among friends, and safe from the English army. He and Hoseason shook hands, and the captain left me alone with the stranger.

He had told the captain that the gold was not his own. Some of the Highlanders had escaped to France after the Forty-Five, but their friends and clansmen in Scotland sometimes managed to find a little money to send them. It was this man's job to take the money across to France, and he did this by travelling secretly to Scotland as often as possible. I thought he was very brave. 'If he's caught by the English army, they'll kill him!' I told myself. I liked the way he seemed to enjoy living dangerously.

When he asked me for whisky, I had to go to ask the captain for the key to the cupboard. I found Hoseason and his officers talking quietly in a corner, and heard them planning to kill the stranger and steal his money. They seemed to think that I would help them, and asked me to bring them secretly some guns from the round-house. I went slowly back to the stranger, not sure what I should do. But when I entered the round-house, and saw him eating his supper, I decided at once.

'They're going to attack you, and murder you!' I told him.

'What!' he cried, jumping up. 'Will ye stand with me, against them?'

'I will! I'm no thief or murderer!' I replied bravely.

'Are ye for King George?'

'More or less,' I answered.

'Well, Mr More-or-less, what's your name?'

'David Balfour,' I said, and then, thinking that a man with so fine a coat must like fine people, I added, 'of Shaws.'

'My name is Stewart,' he said proudly. 'Alan Breck, they call me. And Stewart is a king's name, so it's good enough for me, although I have no name of a farmhouse to add to it.' He looked around him. 'Now, David, I'll take any man who comes in through this door. You must watch the window, and the door behind me, and shoot anyone who tries to enter.'

He gave me a pistol. I was very frightened, but tried hard not to show it. The ship seemed very quiet. Suddenly there was the sound of running feet, and a shout, and then I heard fighting in the doorway. I looked over my shoulder, and saw Mr Shuan, just as Alan drove his sword into the officer's body. Then several men ran at my door. I did not want to hurt them, but it was now or never. I lifted my pistol and shot at them. One man fell, and the others ran away. After a few moments, the sailors attacked again. Alan fought as bravely as before, his sword now red with blood. He was clearly enjoying himself. I had no time to think, but when two more men appeared at the window, I shot them too. Now there were several bodies on the floor, and blood everywhere.

Suddenly I realized that we had won, and that the danger was over. Alan was driving the men out of the round-house like sheep. When he returned, he took me in his arms.

'David!' he cried. 'I love ye like a brother. And oh, man, am I not a grand fighter?' I had to agree. He took a knife from the table and cut a silver button off his blue coat. 'Take this, David. The buttons come from my father, Duncan Stewart. Where ye show that button, the friends of Alan Breck will

*I lifted my pistol and shot at them.*

come to ye.' He spoke as proudly as a king, and I tried not to smile.

We slept in the round-house, one of us keeping watch all night, and the next morning the captain came to speak to us. 'Ye've won the fight, sir,' he said to Alan. 'We're sailing through the Little Minch now, and I'll keep my promise to take ye to Loch Linnhe. But ye've killed my chief officer, Shuan, and without him I can't find my way safely round these rocky coasts. We'll go round the island of Mull, but I warn ye, it'll be dangerous.'

Hoseason was right to be worried. All that day Alan and I sat in the round-house and told each other the stories of our lives, but by night the wind was growing stronger and the sailors found it hard to keep the ship away from the

*A great wave hit the ship.*

dangerous rocks. As we came round Earraid, a small island close to the larger island of Mull, there was a sudden, terrible crash, and we realized that the ship had hit a rock. There was only one thing to do – leave the ship and try to reach land in the ship's boat. But as we were climbing down into the boat, a great wave hit the ship, and knocked some of us into the sea.

I went down and came up again several times. Then, luckily, I managed to find a piece of wood, which helped me to stay up in the water. I looked round, but could not see Alan, or any of the sailors, or the boat. My only hope was to try to swim to Earraid, which I could see, not far away, in the moonlight. It was hard, tiring work, but I reached it, and was very grateful to step on to dry land at last.

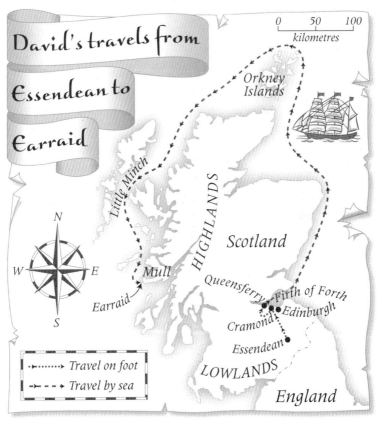

David's travels from Essendean to Earraid

# 3
# David is alone

It was a cold night, so I could not sit down to rest. Instead, I walked up and down on the beach, trying to keep warm. There was no sound except the crash of the waves. I felt very lonely and afraid.

In the morning I climbed a hill, and looked out over the sea, but there was nothing at all on the water. And around me on the island, I could not see any houses or people. I did not like to think what had happened to my friend Alan and the others, and I did not want to look at this emptiness any longer. So I climbed down again, and walked eastwards. I was hoping to find a house, where I could dry my clothes, and get something to eat.

I soon discovered that nobody lived on Earraid. It was too far to swim to Mull, which I could see across the water. I thought perhaps I could wade across, but when I tried it, the water was too deep, and I had to turn back. By now it had started to rain, and I felt very miserable.

Then I remembered the piece of wood, which had already saved my life once. It would help me to get across the sea to Mull! So I walked all the way back to the beach where I had arrived. The piece of wood was in the sea, so I waded into the water to get it. But as I came closer, it moved away from me. And when the water was too deep for me to stand, the piece of wood was still several metres away. I had to leave it, and went back to the beach. It was a terrible moment for me. I was feeling very tired, hungry and thirsty, with no hope of getting away from this lonely island. For the first time since leaving Essendean, I lay down and cried.

I do not want to remember the time that I spent on Earraid. I had nothing with me except my uncle's gold and Alan's silver button, and as I had never lived near the sea, I did not know what to eat or how to fish. In fact, I found some shellfish among the rocks on the coast, and ate them, but I was very sick afterwards. That was the only food that I could find, so I was always hungry on Earraid. All day and all night it rained heavily, but there was no roof or tree on the island, and my clothes were cold and wet on my body.

*I found some shellfish and ate them.*

I chose to spend most of my time in the north of Earraid, on a little hill. From here I could see the old church on the island of Iona, not far away to the west, and smoke from people's houses on Mull, to the east. I used to watch this smoke, and think of the people there, and their comfortable lives. This gave me a little hope, in my lonely life among the rocks and the rain and the cold sea.

Two days passed, and on the third day two things happened. First, I discovered that I had lost almost all my money through a hole in my pocket. I only had three of my uncle's thirty-eight pounds left. But worse was to come. While I was sitting on a rock, looking out over Iona, I suddenly noticed a small boat moving fast through the water. I jumped to my feet and shouted as loudly as I could. The two men in the boat were near enough to hear. They shouted back in Gaelic, and laughed. But the boat did not turn, and sailed on, right in front of my eyes, to Iona.

I could not understand why they did not come to help me. I continued shouting wildly, although I could no longer see them. And then, I lay down and cried for the second time. This time I wasn't sad, but angry, because I thought that they had left me to die alone in that terrible place.

The next morning, I was surprised to see that the same men were sailing towards Earraid from Iona. At once I ran down to the rocky coast to meet them. The boat came near me, but stayed a few metres away in the water. There was a third man in the boat, who was talking and laughing with the others. Then he stood up and spoke fast to me in Gaelic,

*I shouted as loudly as I could.*

which I could not understand. But sometimes he used an English word, and once I heard the word 'tide'. This gave me a flash of hope.

'Do you mean – that when the tide is low . . .?' I cried, and could not finish.

'Yes, yes,' he called back. 'Tide,' and laughed again.

I turned my back on the boat and ran back excitedly to the east of the island, where Earraid was closest to Mull. And sure enough, there was now only a little water between the islands. I was able to wade through it easily, and reached Mull with a happy shout. How stupid of me not to realize that it was possible to get to Mull, twice a day, at low tide! Now I felt very grateful to the boatmen for guessing my problem, and coming back to help me.

I walked towards the smoke that I had seen so often from Earraid, and reached a long, low house built of stone. Outside sat an old man, smoking his pipe in the sun. He spoke a little English, and told me that the officers and sailors from the ship had all arrived there safely a few days before.

'Was one of them dressed in fine clothes?' I asked.

'Aye, there was one like that,' he smiled. 'Ye must be the lad with the silver button!'

'Why, yes!' I said, surprised.

'Well then, your friend says that ye must follow him to the house of his clansman, James Stewart, in Appin.'

He and his wife gave me food and drink, and let me sleep that night in their house. In the morning I thanked them for their kindness, and started my journey to Appin.

I walked across Mull to Torosay, where I took a boat across the water to Lochaline. Then I walked to Kingairlock, where I took another boat across Loch Linnhe to Appin. This took six days, and on my way I met and spoke to a number of travellers. I heard all about Alan's clan, the Stewarts, and their enemies, the Campbells. Although they were both Highland clans, the Campbells and Stewarts had hated each other for years, and now the Campbells were helping the English army drive many Highlanders out of their homes. Indeed, in a day or two, I heard, red-haired Colin Campbell himself was coming to Appin, with King George's soldiers, to drive the Stewarts out and so destroy his enemies. But I heard also of James Stewart, head of the Stewart clan in Appin, and that he and his clansmen would dearly love to see Colin Campbell dead.

People also talked of a man called Alan Breck. Some called him a murderer; others said that he was a brave fighter. He was in danger every time he returned to the Highlands, because the English would pay a good price for him – dead or alive. I listened with interest to everything that they told me. But I liked it best when I heard Alan described as a fine man and an honest Highlander.

When I got out of the boat in Appin, I sat down among some trees to decide what to do next. Should I go on, and join Alan, whose friends were King George's enemies, and whose life was full of danger, or should I go back south again, quietly and safely, to the Lowlands?

As I was thinking, four men on horses came past me on the road. As soon as I saw these men, I decided to continue my adventure, although I cannot explain why. I stopped the first man, who was tall and red-haired.

'Could you tell me the way to James Stewart's house, sir?' I asked.

All the men looked at each other. The red-haired man did not reply, but spoke to one of the others, who looked like a lawyer. 'Is Stewart calling his people together, do ye think?'

The lawyer replied, 'We'd better wait here for the soldiers to join us, before we go any further.'

The red-haired man, I suddenly realized, must be Colin

Campbell himself. 'If you're worried about me,' I said, 'I'm not a Stewart, but a Lowlander, and I'm for King George.'

'That's well said,' replied Campbell, 'but, if I may ask, why is an honest Lowlander like you so far from his home? Today is not a good day for travelling. This is the day when the Appin Stewarts have to leave their farms, and there may be trouble.'

He was turning to speak to the lawyer again, when there came a sudden bang from the hill, and Campbell fell off his horse. 'They've shot me!' he cried, holding his heart.

He died almost immediately. The men's faces were white as they looked down at his body. I saw something move on the hill, and noticed, among the trees, a man with a gun, turning away from the road.

'Look! The murderer!' I cried, and began to run up the hill towards him. He saw me chasing him, and went faster. Soon he disappeared behind a rock, and I could no longer see him. I stopped next to some trees, then I heard a voice below, on the road. The lawyer was shouting to a large number of red-coated soldiers, who had just joined the men around Campbell's dead body. 'Ten pounds if ye catch that lad!' he cried. 'He's one of the murderers! He stopped us in the road, to give the killer a better chance to shoot Campbell!'

Now I felt a new kind of fear. My life was in serious danger, although I had not done anything wrong. My mouth felt dry, and for a moment I could not move. I stood there in the open, on the hill, while the soldiers lifted their guns, ready to shoot.

'Jump in here among the trees,' said a voice near me.

I did not know what I was doing, but I obeyed. As I did so, I heard the banging of the guns, and realized that the soldiers were shooting at me. In the shadow of the trees, I found Alan Breck standing there. It was he who had spoken to me.

*'Look! The murderer!' I cried.*

# 4
# Escape through the heather

We had no time for conversation. 'Come!' Alan said, and started running along the side of the hill, keeping low to the ground. I followed him like a sheep. We ran and ran, faster than I had ever run before, and my heart was beating wildly. Sometimes, to my surprise, Alan straightened his back and showed himself to the soldiers who were chasing us.

After fifteen minutes, Alan stopped, lay flat in the heather, and turned to me. 'Now,' he said, 'this is serious. Do what I do, if ye don't want to die.' And just as fast, but much more carefully and secretly, we went back almost the same way that we had come. At last we arrived back in the wood where I had found Alan.

We fell down in the heather, and lay without moving for a long time. My legs hurt, my head was aching, and I thought I was dead.

Alan was the first to speak. 'Well,' he said, 'that was hot work, David.'

I said nothing. I had seen murder done. I knew that Colin Campbell had been Alan's greatest enemy, and I had found Alan hiding in the wood. Although I didn't think that he had actually shot Campbell, I felt sure that he had planned the killing. I could not look at him.

'Are ye still tired?' he asked.

*We fell down in the heather, and lay without moving.*

'No,' I replied, my face turned away from him, 'no, I'm not tired now. Alan, I can't stay with you, I must leave you. I liked you very much, but we're two different people, that's all.'

'Ye must explain what ye mean by that, David,' said Alan, looking very serious.

'Alan, why do you ask? You know very well that Colin Campbell is lying dead in the road in his own blood.'

Alan was silent for a moment. 'Well, Mr Balfour of Shaws,' he said at last, 'I promise ye that I did not plan the murder, or know anything about it.'

'Thank God for that!' I cried, and offered him my hand.

He did not appear to see it. 'I don't know why ye're so worried about a dead Campbell,' he said.

'I know that you hate their clan, Alan, but taking a life in cold blood is a terrible thing to do. Do you know who did it?'

'I wouldn't recognize him again,' said Alan, shaking his head sadly, 'but I'm good at forgetting, David.'

I had to laugh at that. Then I remembered something. 'But when we were running away, you showed yourself to the soldiers, to give the murderer a chance to escape!'

'Any Highlander would do that. The best place for the lad who shot Colin Campbell is the heather, and we must all do what we can to help him keep away from the soldiers.'

I shook my head at this. These Highlanders were strange, wild people, to be sure. But Alan was ready to die for what he thought was right, and I liked him for that. I offered him my hand again, and this time he took it.

'Now, David,' he said, 'we must escape too. The Campbells will accuse us both of the murder.'

'But we didn't do it!' I cried. 'We can prove that in court!'

'Man, I'm surprised at ye,' said Alan. 'Do ye not know that if a Campbell is killed, the accused has to go to court in Inveraray, in the heart of Campbell country? When the Campbell lawyers have finished with ye, ye'll be dead!'

This frightened me a little. 'All right, Alan,' I said. 'I'll go with you.'

'But remember,' said Alan, 'it'll be a hard life. Ye'll have to sleep in the open air, and ye'll often have an empty stomach. Ye can choose – either live in the heather with me, or die at the hands of the Campbells.'

'That's easy to decide,' I said, and we shook hands on it.

When we looked between the trees, we could just see the red coats of the soldiers, still moving away from us across the hills. Alan smiled, and told me that we would go first to the house of his clansman, James Stewart, and then to the Lowlands. The Campbells and the English soldiers would not think of looking for us there, and Alan could find a place on a ship sailing to France.

We walked for several hours, and arrived that night at a large house in a valley. There were lights in all the windows, and people were running in and out of the open doors. Alan whistled three times, and we were met at the door by a tall, good-looking man of about fifty, who welcomed us in Gaelic.

'James Stewart,' said Alan, 'I'll ask ye to speak in English, because my friend here comes from the Lowlands, and cannot speak Gaelic.'

James spoke politely to me for a few moments, but soon he turned back to Alan, with a very worried look on his face. 'This is a terrible accident,' he said. 'It will bring trouble to all of us!'

'Well, man,' said Alan, 'ye should be grateful that Colin Campbell is dead!'

'Aye,' replied James, 'but he was killed in Appin, remember that, Alan, so it's the Appin Stewarts who'll be accused. And I'm a man with a family!'

I looked around me. Men with white, frightened faces were hurrying here and there, without any clear idea of what they ought to do first. Some were hiding guns and swords, while others were burning papers. When James saw me looking surprised, he explained, 'The soldiers'll search *my* house first, ye see, and I don't want them to find anything.'

We went inside, and met James's wife and children, who were crying in a corner. I felt very sorry for them, but we did not have much time to talk. Alan explained what we needed for our escape, and soon James's men brought us two swords, two pistols, some food, a cooking pot and a bottle of whisky. We needed money too, because Alan had given his gold to another man to take to France. But James had only a little to give us.

'Ye must find a safe place somewhere near,' he said, 'and send me a message. I'll find some more money for ye, and send it to ye. But, Alan,' and here he stopped for a moment, biting his finger worriedly, 'I'll have to accuse ye of killing that Campbell. I'll *have* to! If I don't, they'll accuse *me*! I have to think of myself and my family! Do ye see that?'

'Aye,' said Alan slowly. 'I see that.'

'And I'll have to accuse your friend from the Lowlands too. Ye see that, Alan – say that ye see that!'

Alan's face went red. 'It's hard on me, James! I brought him here, and now my friends accuse him of murder!'

'But just think, Alan, man!' cried James. 'The Campbells will be sure to accuse him. And I have children!'

'Well, sir,' said Alan, turning to me, 'what do ye say? If ye do not agree, I won't let James do it.'

'I cannot understand why we don't accuse the man who *did* kill Campbell,' I replied sharply, 'but accuse me, Mr Stewart, if you like, accuse Alan, accuse King George! I am Alan's friend, and if I can help his friends in any way, I don't mind the danger.'

So that night we started our long journey to the Lowlands. Sometimes we walked, and sometimes we ran. But although we travelled as fast as we could, daylight began to appear before we had found a good hiding-place. We were in the rocky valley of Glencoe, with high mountains on both sides, and a river running fast through the middle. Alan was clearly worried. 'The soldiers will find us easily here,' he said. He looked around, and saw a great rock, about seven metres high. With difficulty we both climbed to the top of it. Then I saw why he had chosen it. The top of the rock was shaped like a plate, and there was room for two or three men to lie there, hidden from people in the valley.

At last Alan smiled. 'Aye,' he said. '*Now* we have a chance. Ye can sleep for a while. I'll watch for soldiers.'

But when I woke up, several hours later, the valley was full of red coats, and Alan was looking worried again. 'If they go up the sides of the mountains, they'll see us,' he said. 'We'll just have to stay here and hope they don't. When it's dark, we'll try to get past them.'

*We lay on the rock, baking in the sun.*

That was a terrible day. We lay on the rock, baking in the sun, with no water, only whisky, to drink. We could hear the English voices of the soldiers all around us, but luckily they did not look up at our rock. In the afternoon, when the soldiers seemed sleepy after their lunch, we decided to try to escape, and we climbed very quietly down from the rock. The soldiers did not notice us as we moved carefully from rock to rock, and soon we were safely in the next valley. That evening we washed ourselves in the river, and ate cold porridge, which is a good meal for a hungry man. We continued walking eastwards all night, over the great dark mountains. Alan was very pleased that we had left the soldiers behind, and whistled happily as he walked.

Before daylight we reached a cave that Alan had used before, and here we stayed hidden for five days. Alan went down one night to the nearest village, to the house of one of his clansmen. He sent this man to James Stewart, to tell him where we were hiding, and after three days the clansman returned, with a purse of money for us and a message from Mrs Stewart. We discovered that James was already in prison, accused of murder, although people were saying that Alan Breck had actually fired the shot. And there was a price of one hundred pounds on my head, as well as on Alan's.

I began to think that I would be safer alone. Alan was very recognizable in his fine French clothes. It was going to be dangerous to stay with Alan, and expensive, too. Mrs Stewart had only managed to send five pounds, and Alan had to travel as far as France. But I still had two pounds, and only needed to reach Queensferry, so I would have to give some of my money to Alan. Staying with Alan meant both danger and expense.

But my honest friend did not think in this way at all. He felt sure that he was helping me. So what could I do, except keep quiet, and hope that everything would be all right?

We started travelling again, across the mountains, and by

daylight came to wild, open moors, covered with purple heather. Because anyone on the hills around us could easily see us when we stood up, we had to walk or run on our hands and feet, like animals. It was another hot summer day, and my back ached badly after a few hours. I wanted a rest and a drink of water, but when we stopped, we saw the red coats of soldiers on one of the hills, and we had to go on.

We walked or ran all day and all night. People who talk of tiredness do not know what the word really means. I did not know who I was or where I was going, and I did not care. I thought that every step would be my last, and I hoped that death would come soon. Alan drove me onwards, and I felt that I hated him, but I was too afraid of him to stop and rest.

When daylight returned, we were stupid with tiredness, and had become careless. Suddenly, three or four wild-looking men jumped out of the heather, and took us prisoner. I was not afraid, only happy to stop running for a moment. But Alan spoke to them in Gaelic.

'These are Cluny Macpherson's men,' he said quietly to me. 'Ye remember him, the head of the Macpherson clan? They fought well against the English in the Forty-Five. After that, he didn't go to France, like the other clan chiefs. No, he's been hiding here ever since, and the soldiers have never managed to find him. His clansmen bring him what he needs.'

We were taken to a cave, well hidden by trees and rocks, and Cluny Macpherson himself came forward to welcome us, like a king in his palace. He seemed to live well in his cave,

*We came to wild, open moors.*

and he offered us an excellent meal, prepared by his cook. But I was too tired to eat, so I lay down at once and slept. In fact, although I did not know it, I was seriously ill, and could not get up for two days. I woke up once, in a kind of fog, to find Cluny and Alan playing cards, and a second time, to hear Alan asking to borrow my money. I was too sick and sleepy to refuse, and gave him my purse.

But when I woke up again, on the third day, I felt much better, although not very strong. I noticed that Alan was looking very ashamed, and I realized at once what had happened.

'David,' he said miserably, 'I've lost all our money at cards, yours as well as mine.'

*I woke up to find Cluny and Alan playing cards.*

'No, no, ye haven't lost it!' cried Cluny. 'Of course I'll give your money back. It was just a game. I wouldn't keep your money. Here!' And he pulled gold coins out of his pocket.

I did not know if it was right to accept the money or not, but we needed it, so I thanked Cluny and put the coins in my purse. But I was very angry with Alan, and as we left Cluny's cave and continued our journey, I refused to speak to him.

At first Alan tried hard to talk to me. He said that he was sorry, and that he loved me like a brother. He was worried about my health, and offered me a hand when we crossed a river or climbed a hill. But after two or three days, when he realized that I was still angry with him, he too became angry, and laughed at me when I fell, or seemed tired.

We travelled by night, through endless rain and strong winds, and slept in the wet heather by day. I was feeling more and more miserable. My illness had returned, and I was beginning to think that this terrible journey would only end in my death. 'Alan will be sorry when I die!' I thought. How childish I was!

Alan continued to laugh at me and call me names, and by the sixth night I had had enough. I stopped and spoke angrily to him. 'Mr Stewart,' I said, 'why do you laugh at me? *I* should laugh at *you*! You may have a king's name, but you're a loser! You spend your life running away! You're not brave enough to fight the Campbells and the English, and win!'

Alan looked sharply at me. 'David!' he said. 'There are things that ye should never say – things that can never be forgotten!'

'If you don't like what I say, I'm ready to fight,' I answered stupidly. I knew that I was not strong enough to hold a sword.

'David!' he cried. 'Are ye crazy? I cannot fight ye! It would be murder!' He pulled out his sword, and looked at me. 'No, I can't, I can't,' he said. And he dropped his sword on the ground.

When I saw how much he loved me, I was no longer angry, only sick, and sorry. I remembered all his kindness to me, and how he had always helped me through difficult times. Now I had lost that friend for ever! My illness seemed to get worse and worse, and I could only just stand. I wanted to say that I was sorry, but I knew it was too late for that. Suddenly I realized that a cry for help was the only way of bringing Alan back to me.

'Alan!' I said, my voice shaking. 'If you cannot help me, I must just die here!' I did not need to pretend.

He looked up quickly, surprised. 'Can ye walk?'

'Not without help. Alan, if I die, will you forget what I said? In my heart, I've always been your friend, you know that.'

'Quiet!' cried Alan. 'Don't talk of dying! David, man, ye know . . .' He could not go on, but put his arm around me.

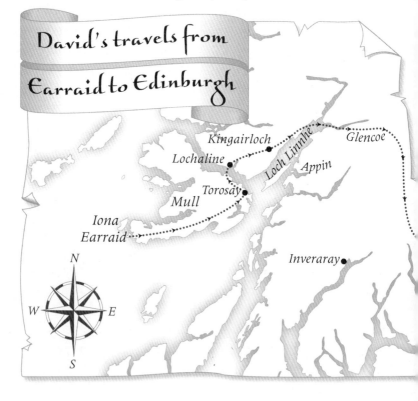

David's travels from Earraid to Edinburgh

'Davie, I'm a bad friend to ye. I didn't remember that ye're just a bairn, I couldn't see that ye were dying on your feet. . .' He was almost crying. 'Hold on to me, Davie, and ye'll be grand.'

He helped me down into the valley to the nearest house, which luckily belonged to a clan who were friendly to the Stewarts. There I lay for several days, unable to move. Alan refused to leave me, and took the greatest care of me. Little by little I got better, with his help, and before a month had passed, we went on our way again.

This time we did not argue. We did not see any more soldiers, and our journey was easier now. We walked through the warm summer nights, ate our porridge, drank our whisky, and slept in the dry heather in the daytime. Now that we were in the Lowlands, we were almost safe, and we both felt happy and hopeful. When we crossed the River Forth by boat from Limekilns, we were only five kilometres from Queensferry, where Mr Rankeillor lived.

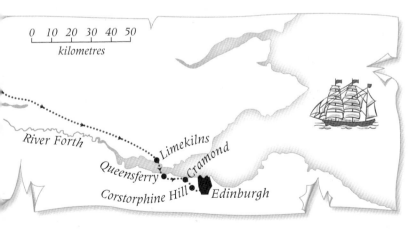

# 5
# David comes home

We decided that Alan would stay hidden in the fields, while I walked to Queensferry to find Mr Rankeillor. Alan promised not to come out until he heard me return. In order to be sure that it was me, he taught me to whistle a little Gaelic song. I have never forgotten it. I think that it will run in my head when I lie dying. Every time it comes to me, I think of that last day of my travels, with Alan whistling opposite me in the grass, while the first light of the sun touched his face.

Soon I arrived in Queensferry. When I saw people looking strangely at me, and realized how dirty my clothes were, I began to feel afraid. Would Mr Rankeillor want to talk to me? How could I prove who I was? I had no papers with me. I was too ashamed to ask any of the townspeople for help, so I walked up and down, not knowing what to do.

By midday I was tired and hungry. I stopped in front of a large house, with clean windows, flowers in the garden, and a dog sitting on the doorstep. Suddenly the door opened, and a large, well-dressed, kind-looking man came out.

'What are you doing here, my lad?' he asked.

'I'm looking for Mr Rankeillor's house, sir,' I answered.

'Well, I'm Rankeillor, and this is my house. Who are you?'

'My name is David Balfour,' I replied.

'David Balfour?' he repeated, and looked closely at me.

*'I'm Rankeillor and this is my house. Who are you?'*

'Come inside, Mr Balfour, and we'll talk.'

In Mr Rankeillor's comfortable sitting-room, I told him the story of my early life, and explained that my uncle had paid Captain Hoseason to kidnap me and take me to sea.

The lawyer listened carefully. 'I heard that Hoseason's ship went down near the island of Mull two months ago,' he said. 'What have you been doing since then?'

'I can easily tell you, sir,' I replied, 'but if I tell you, a friend's life may be in danger. Promise me that you will not get him into trouble, or tell the soldiers about him!'

Although he looked a little worried at first, he promised, and I told him the rest of my adventures. While I talked, his eyes were closed and he seemed to be asleep, but I discovered soon afterwards that he had understood and remembered everything.

When I spoke the name of Alan Breck, he opened his eyes and sat up. 'Don't use unnecessary names, Mr Balfour,' he said. 'A lawyer has to be very careful, when discussing Highlanders. I don't think I heard your friend's name very well. Let's call him – Mr Thomson.'

'Of course,' I thought, 'all over Scotland people are talking about Alan, now that he's accused of the murder of Colin Campbell.' I was sure that Rankeillor had recognized his name. But I just smiled, and continued my story, using the name of Mr Thomson instead of Alan Breck.

'Well, well,' said the lawyer, when I had finished, 'what an exciting adventure! You will have to write it down one day! I had heard of you, Mr David, from your friends in Essendean, who wrote to me when they had no word from you. Your uncle then told me that he had given you money to study in Europe, but I did not think that was true. I'm afraid we all know that Ebenezer Balfour is not a very good or honest man! Then Captain Hoseason appeared, saying that you were lost when his ship went down. But now I understand what really happened, and I know that you are David Balfour.' He put a hand on my shoulder in a fatherly way and continued. 'You'll want to know about the house of Shaws. It's a strange story. When they were young, your father Alexander and his younger brother Ebenezer loved the same girl. Your father was always a kind, loving brother, so when the girl decided to marry *him*, Alexander left Cramond and let Ebenezer have the house and farmland. Well, I think it was a bad mistake. What happened was that your parents were always very poor, and Ebenezer became more and more interested in money. He never married, of course.'

'Well, sir,' I said, 'and now, what will happen?'

'Now that your father is dead,' replied the lawyer, 'you own the house of Shaws and the farms around it. But Ebenezer won't accept that, and it will be expensive if he wants us to prove it in court. In fact, we must stay out of court, if possible. The kidnapping will be difficult to prove, and we don't want people asking questions about your friend Mr Thomson. No, I think that we should leave Ebenezer at Shaws, where he's been for twenty-five years, and ask him to pay you some money every year, instead of giving you the house. What do you think?'

'That sounds excellent to me, sir,' I replied. 'But I think that we *could* accuse my uncle of kidnapping me. It's easier to prove than you think. Listen,' and I described my plan to him.

He was very pleased with it. 'Yes, Mr David, very good! If we can catch Ebenezer like that, he can't refuse to give you *some* of the money that belongs to you!' He called to his secretary, Torrance. 'You must come with us tonight, Torrance. You'll have to listen to the conversation you hear, and write it all down. And bring the Balfour papers with you.' Then he turned to me. 'But if I accept your plan, Mr David, I'll have to meet your friend Mr Thomson, who may be, I only say *may* be, a criminal.' He was silent for a while, thinking deeply, then went on, 'Well, let's talk of something different. Do you know, the other day, I saw Torrance in the street. But because I wasn't wearing my glasses, I didn't recognize him! My own secretary! Ha-ha-ha!' and he laughed happily at himself.

I smiled politely. 'Perhaps he's getting old,' I thought.

But later that evening, when Mr Rankeillor, Torrance and I were walking out of Queensferry, the lawyer suddenly cried out, laughing, 'Well, how stupid of me! I've forgotten my glasses!' And I understood why he had told me the story about Torrance. Now he could meet Alan, a man wanted for murder, and if the soldiers asked him later for information he could say that he never saw Alan clearly and could not possibly recognize him.

When we arrived near Alan's hiding-place, I whistled the little Highland song. When he appeared, we explained to him what we wanted him to do, and he readily agreed. So the four of us continued walking until we reached the house of Shaws.

It was a dark night, and there were no lights in the windows. My uncle was probably in bed. Mr Rankeillor, Torrance and I hid below the steps, near enough to hear any conversation, while Alan went straight up to the door and knocked loudly. After some time my uncle opened his bedroom window, and called down, in a frightened voice, 'What do ye want at this time of night? Who are ye?'

'I do not want to give ye my own name,' replied Alan, 'but I've come to talk to ye about someone called – David.'

'What!' cried my uncle. And after a moment, he said

unhappily, 'Will ye come inside, to discuss – the matter?'

'I will not,' said Alan sharply. 'It's here on this doorstep that we must talk. Come down and speak to me.'

After Ebenezer had thought about it, he decided to do what Alan wanted. It took him a long time to come downstairs, and a longer time to unlock the heavy door, but at last we saw him in the doorway, holding his gun in his shaking hands.

'Now,' said Alan, 'ye're intelligent enough to see that I'm a Highlander. I have friends who live near the island of Mull. Well, it seems that a ship went down near there, and soon afterwards my friends found a lad, half-dead, on the beach. Your nephew, Mr Balfour. Since then they've been taking care of him. And now they'd like to know, Mr Balfour, if ye want him back. Ye'll have to pay, if ye do. My friends are very poor.'

'I don't want him back,' said my uncle. 'He wasn't a good lad. I won't pay a shilling for him!'

'Blood's thicker than water, sir,' said Alan. 'He's your brother's son! But if ye don't want him back, will ye pay us to keep him? And ye'll have to hurry. I'm not waiting here all night!'

'Give me a minute to think, will ye!' cried my uncle.

'In two words, sir, do ye want us to kill or keep the lad?'

'Oh, sir!' cried Ebenezer. 'Don't talk of killing!'

'Well, killing's easier, and quicker, and cheaper.'

'I'm an honest man,' said my uncle, 'and no murderer.'

'Well, well,' replied Alan, 'and now how much will ye pay

*'Do ye want us to kill or keep the lad?' said Alan.*

for us to keep him? First I need to know how much ye paid Hoseason to kidnap the lad. How much was it?'

'Hoseason? Kidnap? What are ye talking about, man?' screamed my uncle, jumping up and down on the doorstep.

'Hoseason himself has told me about it,' said Alan calmly,

'so ye needn't pretend. Just answer the question, or ye'll find my sword in your stomach!'

'Don't get angry!' cried my uncle. 'I gave him twenty pounds, that's all. But to be honest with ye – he was going to sell the lad as a slave, and keep that money, ye see.'

'Thank you, Mr Thomson, that's excellent,' said the lawyer, stepping forward. 'Good evening, Mr Balfour,' he said politely to the old man.

And, 'Good evening, uncle Ebenezer,' said I.

And, 'It's a grand evening, Mr Balfour,' added Torrance.

My uncle said nothing, but stood there on the doorstep with his mouth open. We took him into the kitchen, and sat down to discuss matters. After an hour, it was all decided. My uncle accepted that Shaws belonged to me, but he would stay there during his lifetime. He agreed to pay me money every year, and Mr Rankeillor would check that he did.

We all stayed that night at the house of Shaws. But while Alan and Torrance and Mr Rankeillor slept on the hard beds upstairs, I lay down on the kitchen chests, which now belonged to me. I, who had slept out on the hills for so many days and nights, was now the owner of a large house and several farms. My head was full of exciting plans and ideas, and I found it difficult to sleep.

The next day, while Mr Rankeillor and I were having breakfast together, I talked to him about Alan.

'Mr Thomson is still in danger,' said the lawyer. 'He must leave the country as soon as possible, and stay with his friends in France for a while. I'll give you money to buy him a place on a ship. He'll have to stay hidden until then.'

'And his clansman, James Stewart, who's in prison?' I asked. 'I know he didn't kill Colin Campbell. I *saw* the murderer! I must speak for James Stewart in court!'

'My dear boy,' said Rankeillor, 'it's dangerous for anyone to speak for a Stewart in a Campbell court. But you must do what you think is right. I'll write you a letter to a good lawyer who will be able to help Mr Thomson's clansman.' He stood up. 'Well, I think that we've finished our business here. I must leave now, and go back to my work. Come and see me often, Mr David! Goodbye!'

Alan and I started walking towards Edinburgh, while Mr Rankeillor and Torrance turned back to Queensferry. We talked about what would happen next. Alan was going to hide in the countryside near Edinburgh, until it was safe for him to take a ship to France. When I had found him a place, I would send him a message. Then I planned to go back to the Highlands to help James Stewart return to his family.

Alan and I walked slowly. We were both thinking that soon we would have to leave each other. And we had been through so much together! We stopped when we came to the top of Corstorphine hill, and looked down at Edinburgh. We knew that this was the moment to say goodbye, but we stood there silently for a while.

'Well, goodbye,' said Alan, and held out his hand.

'Goodbye,' I said, and took his hand. Then I went off downhill. I did not look back at him, but I felt very miserable, and wanted to sit down and cry like a baby.

*'Goodbye,' I said, and took his hand.*

Edinburgh was full of noise and traffic and people, but I did not notice any of that. All the time I was thinking of Alan on the hill, and there was an ice-cold feeling inside me.

In the months that followed, I kept Alan's silver button safe and often looked at it, remembering our escape through the heather in the wild Highlands. I felt proud to call Alan Breck Stewart my friend, and wondered if I would ever see him again. When I returned to the Highlands to help his clansman, James, I found that my adventures with the Stewarts were far from finished . . . but that is another story.

# GLOSSARY

**accuse** to say that someone has done something wrong
**attack** to start fighting or hurting someone
**cabin** a room on a ship
**court** the place where judges and lawyers listen to law cases
**fog** when the air is like a cloud and you can't see through it
**Gaelic** the language spoken by some Scottish people
**heather** a plant with small purple flowers, often found on moors
**kidnap** (past tense **kidnapped**) to take someone away from their home and keep them prisoner
**lawyer** someone who helps people with the law or speaks for them in court
**officer** someone on a ship or in the army who gives orders
**porridge** a soft cereal, cooked in milk or water, usually eaten hot
**proud** pleased about something you have or something you did
**prove** to show that something is true
**sharply** crossly, angrily
**shilling** an old British coin (5p in modern money)
**thunder** a very loud noise in the sky when there is a storm
**tide** the rise and fall of the sea that happens twice a day
**wade** to walk through water
**whistle** to make a long high sound by blowing air out between your lips

### SCOTTISH WORDS USED IN THIS STORY

**aye** = yes
**bairn** = child
**clan** = family
**clansman** = family member

**dominie** = schoolteacher
**grand** = fine
**lad** = boy, young man
**ye** = you

# Kidnapped

## ACTIVITIES

## *Before Reading*

1 **Read the story introduction on the first page of the book, and the back cover. What do you know now about the people in the story? Choose Y (Yes) or N (No) for each sentence.**

1 David Balfour comes from the Scottish Highlands. Y/N
2 He leaves home to fight against King George. Y/N
3 His uncle is happy to meet David for the first time. Y/N
4 Life soon becomes dangerous for David. Y/N
5 Alan Breck works for King George. Y/N
6 Alan is a useful friend for David. Y/N
7 David and Alan run away from the English soldiers. Y/N

2 **Read the introduction and the back cover again. Can you guess what is going to happen in the story? Cross out what you think probably won't happen.**

David Balfour learns something very *sad / surprising* about his family. Then he is kidnapped and taken to sea on a ship, where he has to work as a *cabin boy / sailor*. He meets Alan Breck, who teaches him how to *fish / fight*, and becomes his *friend / enemy*. Their ship hits a *rock / boat*, and David swims to *an island / another ship*. While travelling through the *Highlands / Lowlands*, he sees *a murder / an accident*, and is chased by *English soldiers / the police*. He meets *Alan / the ship's captain* again, and together they escape *over the mountains / across the sea*.

# While Reading

**Read Chapter 1. Who said this, and to whom? What, or who, were they talking about?**

1 'That's where I came from, and that's where you must go.'
2 'Blood built it, . . . and blood shall bring it down!'
3 'A promise is a promise.'
4 'They're grand. The stairs are grand.'
5 'Indeed he was! No other reason for killing him!'
6 'Watch out for the old man – he wants to hurt ye.'

**Read Chapter 2, and answer these questions.**

*Why*

1 . . . was David carried up and put in the sailors' cabin?
2 . . . did David have to bring the meals to the round-house?
3 . . . was David afraid of the ship arriving in the Carolinas?
4 . . . did Hoseason and his officers want to kill Alan Breck?
5 . . . did Alan Breck give David a silver button?
6 . . . did David have to swim to Earraid?

**Before you read Chapter 3, can you guess the answers to these questions?**

1 Who does David find on Earraid?
2 What does he find to eat on Earraid?
3 How does he get away from Earraid in the end?

Read Chapter 3. Are these sentences true (T) or false (F)? Rewrite the false sentences with the correct information.

1  David spent three very miserable days on Earraid.
2  He found plenty of things to eat, but lost all his money.
3  He escaped in the end by swimming to Iona.
4  The Stewarts had good reason to hate the Campbells.
5  Colin Campbell was shot on the road in front of David.
6  David ran up the hill because he was chasing Alan Breck.

Before you read Chapter 4, what do you think happens next? Choose Y (Yes) or N (No) for each of these ideas.

1  David goes back down to the road and gets arrested. Y/N
2  The soldiers arrest Alan, but David escapes. Y/N
3  David and Alan both escape from the soldiers. Y/N
4  David and Alan both escape, but David is shot. Y/N
5  David finds out that it was Alan who shot Campbell. Y/N

Read Chapter 4, and answer these questions.

1  Why did Alan show himself to the soldiers chasing them?
2  What made David decide to go on the run with Alan?
3  What was Alan's plan of escape?
4  Why was James Stewart so worried?
5  What was the message sent later by James Stewart's wife?
6  Why didn't David care when he was taken prisoner?
7  What happened to all Alan's and David's money?
8  What did Alan do when David refused to speak to him?
9  When did Alan realize how ill David was?

**Before you read Chapter 5 (*David comes home*), can you guess how the story ends? Choose some of these ideas.**

1 David becomes the owner of the Balfour house and land.
2 Alan tries to make Ebenezer give him some money.
3 Ebenezer goes to prison for arranging David's kidnap.
4 Alan asks David to go to France with him.
5 David is very sad when he has to say goodbye to Alan.

**Read Chapter 5. Match these halves of sentences and use the linking words to make a paragraph of seven sentences. (Use each linking word once.)**

*after / and / because / but / so / that / when / while / until*

1 _____ Alan stayed hidden in the fields, . . .
2 The lawyer was not sure who David really was, . . .
3 Then, with Alan's help, they made Ebenezer say aloud . . .
4 _____ his crime was now proved, . . .
5 _____ David lay down to sleep that night, . . .
6 _____ Alan was still in danger, . . .
7 _____ Alan had left, David kept the silver button safe, . . .

8 _____ the boy had described all his adventures to him.
9 _____ he had to leave for France as soon as possible.
10 David walked to Queensferry to find Mr Rankeillor.
11 _____ felt proud to call Alan Breck Stewart his friend.
12 Ebenezer had to agree to pay David money every year.
13 _____ he had paid Hoseason to kidnap David.
14 he was rich, for the first time in his life.

## *After Reading*

1 **Who's who in the story? Match each character to three of the notes, and join the information together to make six short paragraphs, one about each person.**

*Ebenezer Balfour / Captain Hoseason / Alan Breck / Colin Campbell / James Stewart / Mr Rankeillor*

1 a man with an open, sunburnt face and bright, amused eyes
2 a tall, red-haired man
3 a large, well-dressed, kind-looking man
4 a Gaelic-speaking man of about fifty
5 a dark, serious-looking man
6 a small, mean-looking, white-faced old man

7 a ship's captain / a hard man
8 only interested in money / tried twice to get David killed
9 a clansman of Alan's / wife and children
10 an honest lawyer / had known David's father
11 a brave Highlander / fought for his country in 1745
12 hated by the Stewarts / working with the English

13 travelled often to France, carrying gold for other people
14 wanted to keep the family house and land for himself
15 was shot on the road to Appin by a Highlander
16 wanted the right person to inherit the house of Shaws
17 agreed to kidnap David and sell him as a slave in America
18 did not want the Campbells to accuse him of murder

2 Here are extracts from seven conversations. Who is speaking, and to whom? What is happening in the story at this moment? When you have answered these questions, put the conversations in the right order, as they happened in the story.

1 'What do ye say, Alan, to a game or two of cards? Just to pass the time, while your friend is resting. We could play for a shilling a game, if you like, to make it interesting.'

2 'You see, sir, what we have to do is make him say that he paid Captain Hoseason to kidnap me. And if several of us are listening, he can't pretend later that he didn't say it!'

3 'Do what ye like with him, captain. Throw him in the sea, sell him as a slave – it's all the same to me. I never want to see the boy again!'

4 'Watch out for the lad, will ye? He'll have a silver button to show ye, so ye'll know it's him. He'll have to find his own way to James's house, if he gets this far.'

5 'Just listen, Davie lad. Now ye must try it. It's an old Gaelic song from the West Highlands, this one. Yes, that's good. Ye've nearly got it. Try once more.'

6 'And tell him they've taken James away to prison. Me and the bairns are on our own now! And warn him there's a price of a hundred pounds on his head and his friend's!'

7 'It'll be easy, gentlemen. We'll wait until he's asleep and then we'll jump on him! We'll each need a pistol from the round-house . . .'

3 Here are two new titles for each chapter. Put the titles into two groups – places and people – and then put the titles in each group in the right order for the story.

Escape through the Highlands    Meeting Uncle Ebenezer

Who is Alan Breck?    Alan has to leave

From Essendean to Cramond    By sea to Earraid

A lonely journey to Appin    A Campbell is murdered

On the run with Alan Breck    Back to the house of Shaws

4 There are 20 words (4 letters or longer) from the story in this word search. Find the words (they go from left to right, and from top to bottom), and draw lines through them.

| Y | H | E | A | T | H | E | R | O | U | M | A | T | Y |
|---|---|---|---|---|---|---|---|---|---|---|---|---|---|
| H | I | A | P | V | B | E | A | W | A | D | E | I | K |
| I | G | I | O | L | O | W | L | A | N | D | S | D | N |
| W | H | S | R | S | A | A | A | G | C | S | A | E | N |
| H | L | L | R | H | T | V | W | A | O | M | I | E | B |
| I | A | A | I | I | U | E | Y | G | A | E | L | I | C |
| S | N | N | D | P | T | Y | E | O | S | U | O | R | A |
| K | D | D | G | C | O | U | R | T | T | E | R | A | B |
| Y | S | H | E | L | L | F | I | S | H | L | O | S | I |
| E | R | P | R | O | V | E | C | A | P | T | A | I | N |

1 How many of the words from the word search are connected with the sea, in some way or another?

2 There are also 6 words which are connected with Scotland. Which words are they? Can you explain the connection?

66

5 **Look at the word search again, and write down all the letters without a line through them. Begin with the first line, and go across each line to the end. You should have 34 letters, which will make a sentence of 10 words.**

　1　What is the sentence, and who said it, to whom?

　2　Why was it a terrible thing to say?

　3　Did the speaker really mean it?

　4　Why did he say it?

　5　What happened next?

6 **'Blood's thicker than water.' This saying is used by both Ebenezer and Alan. Answer these questions about it.**

　1　Does the saying have both these meanings, or just one of them?

　　a)　Family relationships are the strongest ones.

　　b)　Your family is more important than your friends.

　2　What do *you* think? Do you think that somebody's family should always come first? Or their friends? Why?

7 **What did you think about the characters in this story? Complete these sentences in your own words.**

　•　I liked ____ when / because _____

　•　I did not like ____ when / because _____

　•　I was afraid for ____ when _____

　•　I was sorry for ____ when _____

　•　I was pleased when _____

　•　I wanted ____ to _____

　•　The character I liked best was ____, because _____

# ABOUT THE AUTHOR

Robert Louis Stevenson was born in Edinburgh, in Scotland, in 1850. His father was an engineer, and in 1867 Robert went to Edinburgh University to study engineering himself. He found that engineering did not interest him, so he trained to be a lawyer, but in fact he had already decided to become a writer. He met his future wife in France. Fanny was American, ten years older than Stevenson, and a married woman with two children. They fell in love, and after her divorce, she and Stevenson were married in 1880, in San Francisco in the USA.

Stevenson liked to travel, although much of the time his health was poor. In 1888, he and Fanny went to live on the Pacific island of Samoa because the weather there was good for Stevenson's health. The islanders called him 'The Teller of Tales'. He died suddenly on Samoa in 1894, aged only 44.

Stevenson's most famous titles include *Dr Jekyll and Mr Hyde* (1886) and his exciting adventure stories, *Treasure Island* (1883) and *Kidnapped* (1886). In *Kidnapped* he used his experience as a young man, when he travelled round Scotland, looking at the lighthouses designed by his father. During one journey in 1870, he spent three weeks on the island of Earraid, where David Balfour is shipwrecked in the story. The novel also shows Stevenson's interest in Scottish history. The murder of Colin Campbell was a real historical event, and Alan Breck was a real person, who was suspected of the murder – although it was James Stewart who was later hanged for it. The adventures of the Stewarts are continued in *Catriona* (1893), in which David falls in love for the first time.

# OXFORD BOOKWORMS LIBRARY

*Classics • Crime & Mystery • Factfiles • Fantasy & Horror*
*Human Interest • Playscripts • Thriller & Adventure*
*True Stories • World Stories*

The OXFORD BOOKWORMS LIBRARY provides enjoyable reading in English, with a wide range of classic and modern fiction, non-fiction, and plays. It includes original and adapted texts in seven carefully graded language stages, which take learners from beginner to advanced level. An overview is given on the next pages.

All Stage 1 titles are available as audio recordings, as well as over eighty other titles from Starter to Stage 6. All Starters and many titles at Stages 1 to 4 are specially recommended for younger learners. Every Bookworm is illustrated, and Starters and Factfiles have full-colour illustrations.

The OXFORD BOOKWORMS LIBRARY also offers extensive support. Each book contains an introduction to the story, notes about the author, a glossary, and activities. Additional resources include tests and worksheets, and answers for these and for the activities in the books. There is advice on running a class library, using audio recordings, and the many ways of using Oxford Bookworms in reading programmes. Resource materials are available on the website <www.oup.com/elt/bookworms>.

The *Oxford Bookworms Collection* is a series for advanced learners. It consists of volumes of short stories by well-known authors, both classic and modern. Texts are not abridged or adapted in any way, but carefully selected to be accessible to the advanced student.

———————————————

You can find details and a full list of titles in the *Oxford Bookworms Library Catalogue* and *Oxford English Language Teaching Catalogues*, and on the website <www.oup.com/elt/bookworms>.

# THE OXFORD BOOKWORMS LIBRARY
## GRADING AND SAMPLE EXTRACTS

### STARTER • 250 HEADWORDS

present simple – present continuous – imperative –
*can/cannot, must* – *going to* (future) – simple gerunds …

Her phone is ringing – but where is it?

Sally gets out of bed and looks in her bag. No phone. She looks under the bed. No phone. Then she looks behind the door. There is her phone. Sally picks up her phone and answers it. *Sally's Phone*

### STAGE 1 • 400 HEADWORDS

… past simple – coordination with *and*, *but*, *or* –
subordination with *before*, *after*, *when*, *because*, *so* …

I knew him in Persia. He was a famous builder and I worked with him there. For a time I was his friend, but not for long. When he came to Paris, I came after him – I wanted to watch him. He was a very clever, very dangerous man. *The Phantom of the Opera*

### STAGE 2 • 700 HEADWORDS

… present perfect – *will* (future) – *(don't) have to, must not, could* –
comparison of adjectives – simple *if* clauses – past continuous –
tag questions – *ask/tell* + infinitive …

While I was writing these words in my diary, I decided what to do. I must try to escape. I shall try to get down the wall outside. The window is high above the ground, but I have to try. I shall take some of the gold with me – if I escape, perhaps it will be helpful later. *Dracula*

... *should, may* – present perfect continuous – *used to* – past perfect –
causative – relative clauses – indirect statements ...

Of course, it was most important that no one should see
Colin, Mary, or Dickon entering the secret garden. So Colin
gave orders to the gardeners that they must all keep away
from that part of the garden in future. *The Secret Garden*

### STAGE 4 • 1400 HEADWORDS

... past perfect continuous – passive (simple forms) –
*would* conditional clauses – indirect questions –
relatives with *where/when* – gerunds after prepositions/phrases ...

I was glad. Now Hyde could not show his face to the world
again. If he did, every honest man in London would be proud
to report him to the police. *Dr Jekyll and Mr Hyde*

### STAGE 5 • 1800 HEADWORDS

... future continuous – future perfect –
passive (modals, continuous forms) –
*would have* conditional clauses – modals + perfect infinitive ...

If he had spoken Estella's name, I would have hit him. I was so
angry with him, and so depressed about my future, that I could
not eat the breakfast. Instead I went straight to the old house.
*Great Expectations*

### STAGE 6 • 2500 HEADWORDS

... passive (infinitives, gerunds) – advanced modal meanings –
clauses of concession, condition

When I stepped up to the piano, I was confident. It was as if I
knew that the prodigy side of me really did exist. And when I
started to play, I was so caught up in how lovely I looked that
I didn't worry how I would sound. *The Joy Luck Club*

# The Crown of Violet

### GEOFFREY TREASE

*Retold by John Escott*

High up on a stone seat in the great open-air theatre of Athens, Alexis, son of Leon, watches the Festival of Plays – and dreams of seeing his own play on that famous Stage.

So, as the summer passes, Alexis writes his play for the next year's Festival. But then, with his friend Corinna, he learns that Athens has enemies – enemies who do not like Athenian democracy, and who are planning a revolution to end it all . . .

# Rabbit-Proof Fence

### DORIS PILKINGTON GARIMARA

*Retold by Jennifer Bassett*

Fourteen-year-old Molly and her cousins Daisy and Gracie were mixed-race Aborigines. In 1931 they were taken away from their families and sent to a camp to be trained as good 'white' Australians. They were told to forget their mothers, their language, their home.

But Molly would not forget. She and her cousins escaped and walked back to Jigalong, 1600 kilometres away, following the rabbit-proof fence north across Western Australia to their desert home.

*Rabbit-Proof Fence* is the true story of that walk, told by Molly's daughter, Doris. It is also a prize-winning film.